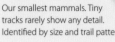

FRONT: L ⁷⁄₁₆"–⁷⁄₁₆" ; W ⁷⁄₁₆"–⁷⁄₁₆"
HIND: L ³⁄₁₆"–⁷⁄₁₆"; W ³⁄₁₆"–⁵⁄₁₆"

Our smallest mammals. Tiny tracks rarely show any detail. Identified by size and trail patterns.

Moles

FRONT: L ³⁄₈"–⅝"; W ³⁄₈"–⅝"
HIND: L ¼"–½"; W ¼"–½"

Tracks of this fossorial mammal are rarely seen. Digging signs are quite obvious.

Eastern Harvest Mouse

FRONT: L ¼"–³⁄₈"; W ¼"–⁵⁄₁₆"
HIND: L ¼"–½"; W ³⁄₁₆"–⁵⁄₁₆"

Our smallest mouse. The "thumb" on the hind foot is set farther back than in other mice. Found only in MD.

House Mouse

FRONT: L ¼"–½"; W ⁵⁄₁₆"–³⁄₈"
HIND: L ⁵⁄₁₆"–¾"; W ⁵⁄₁₆"–⁷⁄₁₆"

Hind tracks are larger than the front tracks, unlike in native mice. Common in and around buildings.

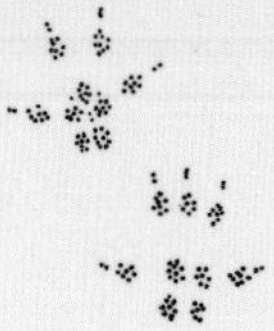

White-footed Mice

FRONT: L ¼"–½"; W ⁵⁄₁₆"–½"
HIND: L ¼"–⁹⁄₁₆"; W ⁵⁄₁₆"–½"

Very common. Bulbous toe pads. Trail patterns resemble that of a miniature squirrel.

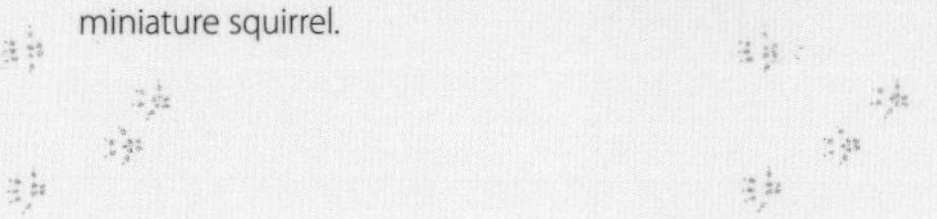

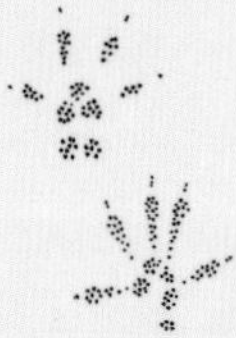

Voles & Lemmings

FRONT: L ¼"–½"; W ¼"–½"
HIND: L ¼"–⅝"; W ¼"–½"

Common around fresh vegetation. Long, fingery toes. Usually walks or trots rather than bound.

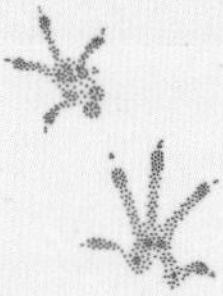

Jumping Mice

FRONT: L ⅜"–⅝"; W ⅜"–⅝"
HIND: L ½"–1⅛"; W ⅜"–¾"

Have extremely long, slender toes. May make very long leaps. Hibernates through the winter in colder climates.

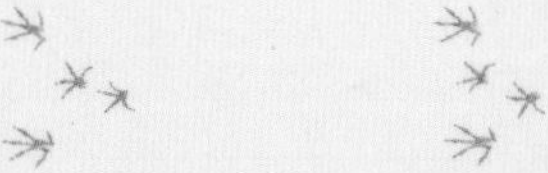

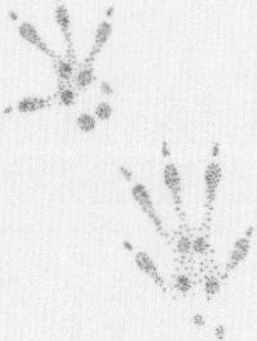

Marsh Rice Rat

FRONT: L ½"–¾"; W ½"–⅝"
HIND: L ¹¹⁄₁₆"–1¼"; W ⁹⁄₁₆"–¾"

Has long, slender toes and small pads. Found in wet habitats in DE, MD, NJ, and eastern PA.

Tiny Mammals

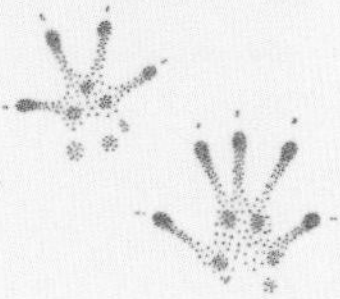

Norway Rat

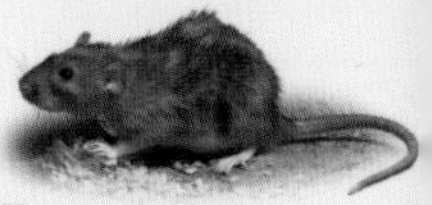

FRONT: L 1/2"–13/16"; W 1/2"–13/16"
HIND: L 5/8"–1 1/4"; W 5/8"–1 1/8"

Most common around buildings.
Very similar to Rice Rat tracks; use habitat and behavior to distinguish between them.

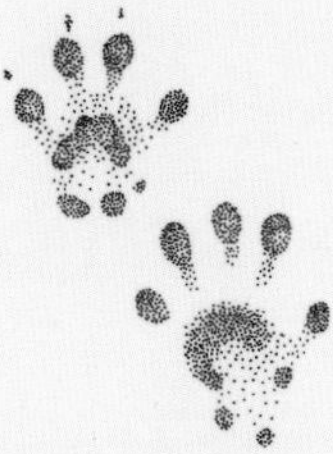

Allegheny Woodrat

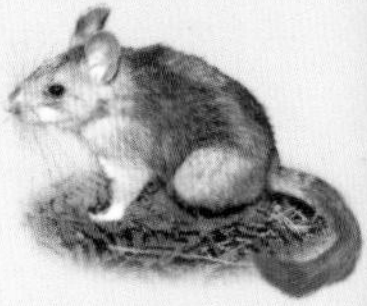

FRONT: L 3/8"–7/8"; W 3/8"–3/4"
HIND: L 1/2"–1 1/4"; W 1/2"–7/8"

More bulbous toe pads than other rats. Builds enormous stick nests. Lives in the mountains of MD, PA and northeastern NJ.

Squirrels

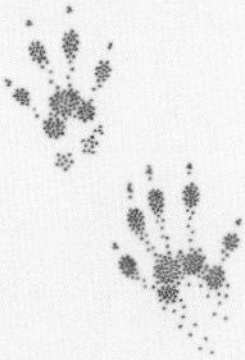

Eastern Chipmunk

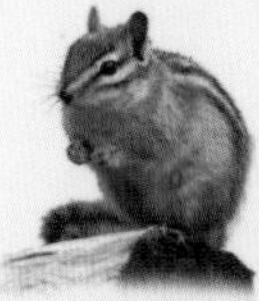

FRONT: L 1/2"–7/8"; W 3/8"–3/4"
HIND: L 1/2"–1"; W 1/2"–7/8"

Tracks and trails are similar to those of tree squirrels, but in miniature. Toes tend to splay less than in similarly sized rat tracks.

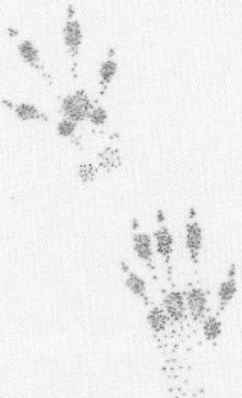

Flying Squirrels

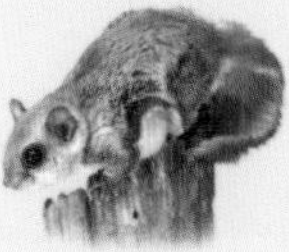

FRONT: L 3/8"–3/4"; W 3/8"–3/4"
HIND: L 1/2"–1 3/8"; W 3/8"–7/8"

Smallest squirrel tracks in the Northeast. Wide-set front feet create "boxy" trail patterns.

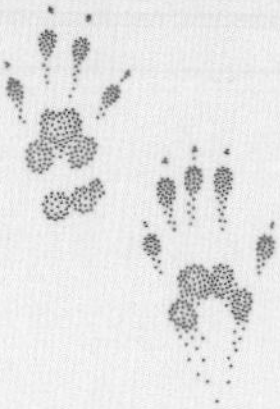

Red Squirrel

FRONT: L ⅞"–1¼"; W ½"–1"
HIND: L 1"–2"; W ¾"–1¼"

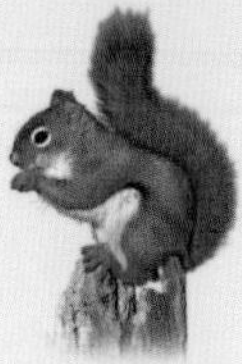

Long, slender toes make tracks appear more delicate than other squirrel tracks. Larger tracks than flying squirrels and smaller than those of gray squirrels.

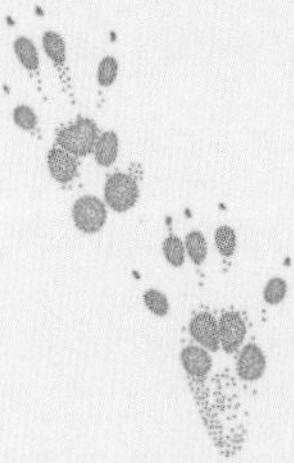

Eastern Gray Squirrel

FRONT: L 1"–1⅝"; W ½"–1¼"
HIND: L 1"–2½"; W ⅞"–1½"

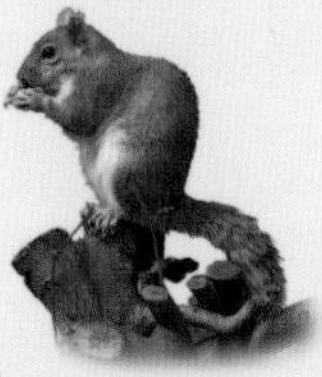

These familiar animals leave abundant tracks. Long toes and clearly defined pads distinguish them from rabbit tracks.

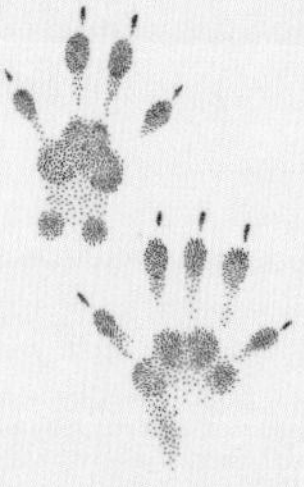

Eastern Fox Squirrel

FRONT: L 1¼"–1¾"; W ¾"–1½"
HIND: L 1½"–2¾"; W 1"–1¾"

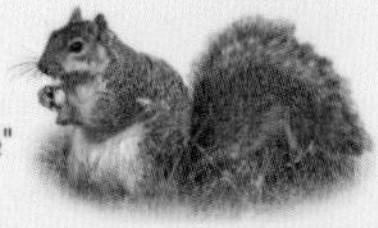

Our largest tree squirrel. Ventures farther from trees and walks more often than gray squirrels. Lives in DE, MD, parts of NY and eastern PA.

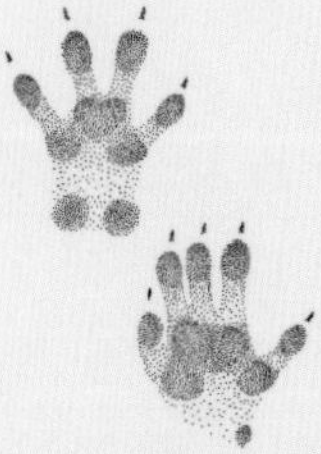

Woodchuck

FRONT: L 1⅝"–2½"; W 1⅛"–1⅞"
HIND: L 1⅝"–2¾"; W 1¼"–1⅞"

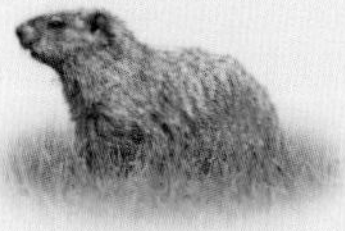

Large, stubby, squirrel-like tracks. Usually walks rather than bounds.

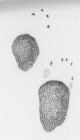

North American Porcupine

FRONT: L 2¼"–3¼"; **W** 1½"–1⅞"
HIND: L 2¾"–4"; **W** 1¼"–2"

Oval tracks with a unique "pebbly" texture. Prominent claws, but toes rarely show. Highly arboreal.

Muskrat

FRONT: L 1"–1½"; **W** 1"–1½"
HIND: L 1½"–2½"; **W** 1⅜"–2¼"

Usually found near water. Prominent claws. Long hind toes are fringed with stiff hairs.

Nutria

FRONT: L 1"–2⅜"; **W** 1⅛"–2¼"
HIND: L 2⅛"–4½"; **W** 2"–3"

Non-native aquatic rodent. Tracks are similar to beaver, but smaller. Range is expanding from the Chesapeake to southern NJ & PA.

American Beaver

FRONT: L 2"–3½"; **W** 1½"–3"
HIND: L 4½"–7"; **W** 3"–5"

Clear hind prints are unmistakable. Trails usually lead to or from water.

Rabbits

Cottontail Rabbits

FRONT: L ⅞"–1¾"; W ⅝"–1¼"
HIND: L 1¼"–3¼"; W ¾"–1⅝"

Very common. Egg-shaped tracks. Distinctive triangular-shaped bounding trail pattern.

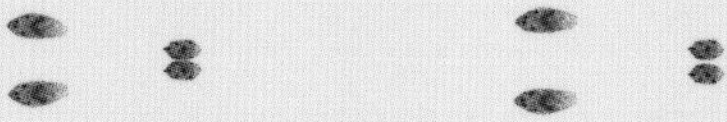

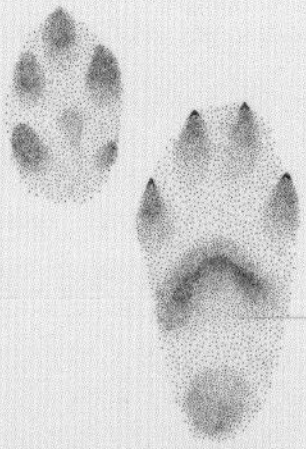

Snowshoe Hare

FRONT: L 1¾"–3"; W 1¼"–2¼"
HIND: L 3"–5"; W 1½"–4½"

Tracks and trails similar to cottontails, but feet are much larger. Hind feet may splay widely.

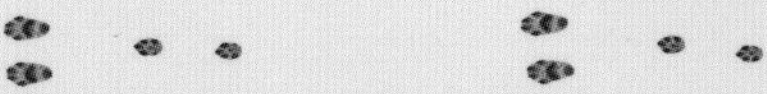

Skunks

Eastern Spotted Skunk

FRONT: L 1"–1⅜"; W ¾"–1"
HIND: L ¾"–1¼"; W ⅝"–1⅛"

Tracks have a clean, compact look. Prominent claws. Irregular gaits. Extremely rare. Found in the mountains of MD and southern PA.

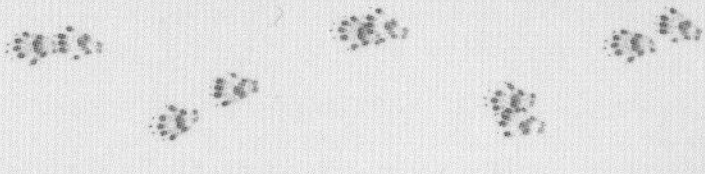

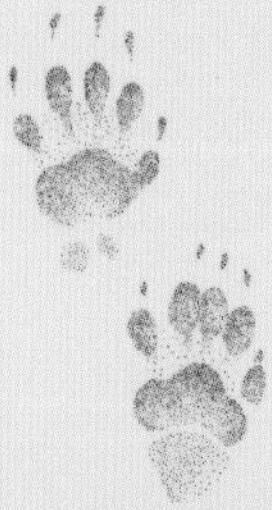

Striped Skunk

FRONT: L ⅞"–1¾"; W ⅞"–1¼"
HIND: L 1"–1¾"; W ⅞"–1¼"

Prominent claws. Toes never splay. Trails resemble those of a miniature bear.

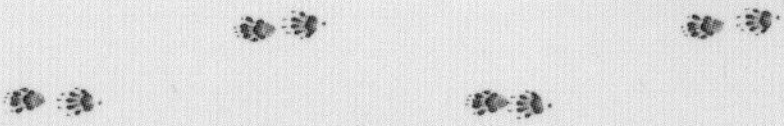

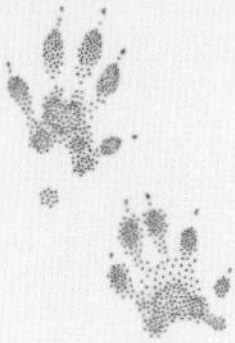

Weasels

FRONT: L 5/16"–1/2"; W 5/16"–1/2"
HIND: L 5/16"–1/2"; W 5/16"–1/2"

Our smallest carnivores.
Typical track pattern is a 2x2
bound with long, irregular strides.

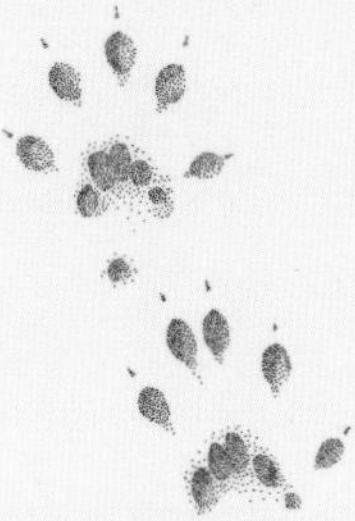

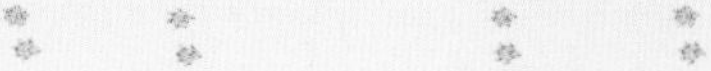

American Mink

FRONT: L 1"–1¾"; W ¾"–1⅝"
HIND: L ¾"–1½"; W ⅞"–1⅝"

Usually found close to water.
Individual tracks may resemble those of tree squirrels, but track patterns are usually distinctive.

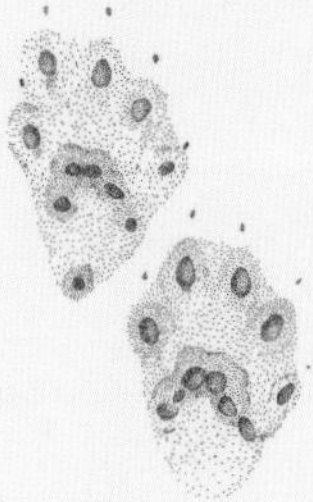

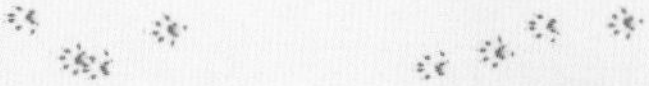

American Marten

FRONT: L 1½"–2¾"; W 1⅜"–2½"
HIND: L 1½"–2⅝"; W 1⅜"–2½"

Thick fur often blurs palm and toe pads.
Highly arboreal–trails often end at the
base of a tree. Found in northern ME.

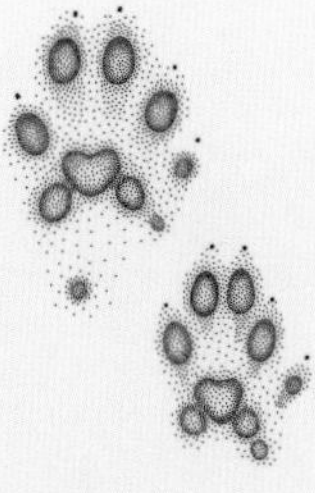

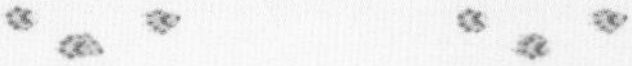

Fisher

FRONT: L 2⅛"–3½"; W 2"–3¼"
HIND: L 2"–3"; W 1¾"–3"

Front tracks larger than hind.
Large negative space and slender
palm help distinguish from canines and felines.

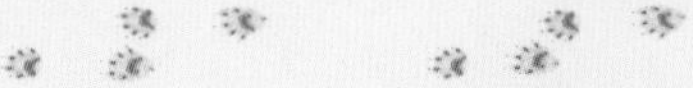

River Otter

FRONT: L 2"–3"; W 1⅞"–3"
HIND: L 2¼"–3¾"; W 2⅛"–3½"

Usually found near water,
often in small groups. Webbing rarely
shows clearly in tracks. Trails may include slides.

Gray Fox

FRONT: L 1¼"–1¾"; W 1¼"–1¾"
HIND: L 1⅛"–1¾"; W 1"–1⅝"

Our smallest wild canine.
Tracks appear rounder and
more cat-like than the red fox's.
Semi-retractable claws may not register.

Red Fox

FRONT: L 1¾"–2½"; W 1½"–2⅛"
HIND: L 1½"–2½"; W 1¼"–1⅞"

Heavy fur often makes features
less distinct than those of
other canids. Thin "bar" may show
in the palm, especially in the front track.

Coyote

FRONT: L 2"–3"; W 1½"–2¾"
HIND: L 2"–3"; W 1⅜"–2¼"

Compared to domestic dogs,
toes tend to register deeper
than the palm; the slender
claws typically point straight ahead.

Domestic Dog

**Range from smaller than a gray fox's
to larger than a coyote's**

Ubiquitous. Various breeds. Tracks
range from coyote-like to nearly
round. Stout claws often prominent,
but trimmed nails may not show.

Dogs

Domestic Dog (Cat-footed)

Range from smaller than a gray fox's to larger than a coyote's

Some dog breeds leave round, cat-like tracks. Trimmed nails may not show. More symmetrical than cat tracks, with a smaller palm.

Cats

House Cat
FRONT: L 1"–1⅝"; W 1"–1¾"
HIND: L 1⅛"–1⅝"; W ⅞"–1⅝"

Tracks are round with a large palm pad. Front and hind track more similar than in bobcats. Claws rarely show.

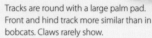

Bobcat
FRONT: L 1½"–2½"; W 1½"–2½"
HIND: L 1½"–2½"; W 1¼"–2¼"

Asymmetrical front track may be wider than it is long. Hind track is narrower, more symmetrical, and has a taller negative space.

Canada Lynx
FRONT: L 2¾"–4"; W 2⅜"–4½"
HIND: L 2¾"–4"; W 2½"–4¼"

Large, round tracks. Heavily furred feet can make pads look small and indistinct. Found in northern ME, NH and VT.

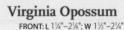

Virginia Opossum

FRONT: L 1¾"–2⅛"; W 1½"–2¼"
HIND: L 1½"–2½"; W 1½"–2⅝"

Front track has starlike shape. Hind track resembles a human hand. Tracks often overlap, creating a jumble of pads.

Northern Raccoon

FRONT: L 1¾"–2¾"; W 1½"–2¾"
HIND: L 2"–2¾"; W 1½"–2¾"

Highly variable tracks often resemble human handprints. Sometimes mistaken for otter tracks, but distinctive 2x2 track pattern is diagnostic.

Black Bear

FRONT: L 3½"–6"; W 3½"–5½"
HIND: L 5"–8"; W 3½"–5¾"

Five toes and robust palm pads. Very large. Clear prints are unmistakable. Typically walks with front feet turned in.

Wild Boar

FRONT: L 2"–2½"; W 2⅛"–2¾"
HIND: L 1¾"–2¼"; W 1¾"–2¼"

Leaves prominent signs when rooting for food. Turns up earth and does considerable damage to vegetation. Uncommon, but reported in NH, NJ, NY, PA and VT.

White-tailed Deer

FRONT: L 2"–3½"; W 1⅝"–2¾"
HIND: L 1⅞"–3¼"; W 1½"–2½"

Extremely abundant. Distinctive and familiar heart-shaped track.

Moose

FRONT: L 4½"–7"; W 3¾"–5¾"
HIND: L 4¼"–6½"; W 3½"–5"

Enormous heart-shaped tracks are unmistakable. Similar to deer tracks, but much larger. Found in northern ME, NH, VT and northeastern NY.

Horse

FRONT: L 4¾"–5½"; W 4¼"–5¼"
HIND: L 4½"–5¼"; W 4"–4¾"

Large, round, single-toed tracks are unmistakable.

Domestic Cow

FRONT: L 2½"–4¾"; W 2¼"–5¾"
HIND: L 2½"–4¾"; W 2¼"–4¾"

Large, rounded, two-toed tracks are unmistakable in our region. In the Northeast, found almost exclusively on private farmland.

American Robin

L 1¾"–2⅛"; **W** ¾"–1"

Curved toes give tracks a
"peeling banana" shape.
Large pad on the hallux.
Runs and skips, with frequent stops.

Mourning Dove

L 1⅝"–1⅞"; **W** 1"–1¼"

Squat, wide tracks. Outer toe is
straight; other toes curve inward.
Walks with short steps.

American Crow

L 2¾"–3½"; **W** 1⅛"–1⅝"

Large classic bird track with
somewhat bulbous toes. Central
and innermost toes are nearly
parallel. Walks, hops, and skips.

Bald Eagle

L 6"–7½"; **W** 3¼"–5"

Extremely large classic bird track
with robust, bulbous toes and
prominent claws. Walks.

Great Blue Heron

L 6"–8½"; **W** 4"–6"

Largest bird track in the
Northeast. Long toes are
smooth and narrow. Walks.

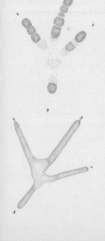

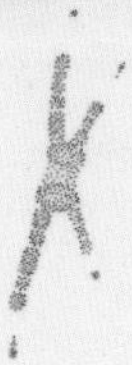

Northern Flicker

L 1¾"–2½"; **W** ⅜"–⅝"

Narrow K-shaped tracks. Often forages on the ground for ants. Hops.

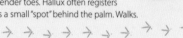

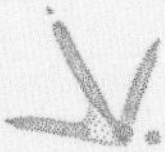

Spotted Sandpiper

L ⅞"–1¼"; **W** 1⅛"–1⅜"

Symmetrical tracks with smooth, slender toes. Hallux often registers as a small "spot" behind the palm. Walks.

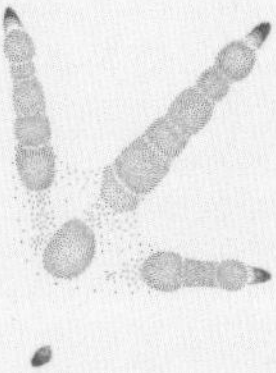

Wild Turkey

L 3⅜"–5"; **W** 3⅝"–5¼"

Large game bird track with bulbous toes and blunt nails. Palm and hallux usually register. Partial webbing sometimes visible. Walks.

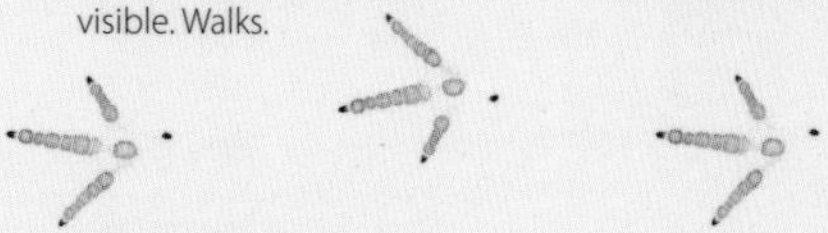

Ring-billed Gull

L 1⅞"–2¼"; **W** 2"–2⅜"

Outer toes strongly curved. Webbing usually visible. Hallux is smaller than in duck tracks and rarely registers. Palm registers about half the time. Walks.

Canada Goose

L 3¾"–4½"; **W** 3¼"–5"

Outer toes are curved, unlike a turkey's. Webbing visible. Duck tracks are similar, but usually show a hallux. Walks.

Painted Turtle

FRONT: L ⁹⁄₁₆"–1"; W ¹¹⁄₁₆"–1³⁄₁₆"
HIND: L ¹³⁄₁₆"–1⁵⁄₁₆"; W ⁵⁄₈"–⁷⁄₈"

Front feet are wider than they are long, while hind feet are longer than wide. Often only the claws register clearly. Most common near ponds.

Common Five-lined Skink

FRONT: L ¼"–½"; W ¼"–½"
HIND: L ½"–1¼"; W ³⁄₈"–¾"

Small. Clear prints are rare. Most trails show prominent belly drag. Prefers moist, wooded habitat, but may reside in buildings.

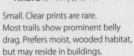

Eastern Newt

FRONT: L ⁵⁄₁₆"–³⁄₈"; W ³⁄₁₆"–⁵⁄₁₆"
HIND: L ⁵⁄₁₆"–³⁄₈"; W ⁵⁄₁₆"–³⁄₈"

Small. Greatly reduced outer toes give these tracks a distinctive "trident" shape, unique among salamanders of the Northeast.

American Bullfrog

FRONT: L 2"–2¾"; W ⅞"–1¼"
HIND: L 2¼"–3⅞"; W 1"–2½"

Our largest frog. Leaves complete tracks more often than smaller frogs and toads. Usually found within one bound length of the water's edge.

Individual Track Identification

If possible, locate both front and hind tracks of the animal. Then use these four steps to help identify the tracks:

1. Study the overall shape of the track.
2. Count the number of toes.
3. Look at the claw marks.
4. Measure the size of the track.

STEP 1. STUDY THE OVERALL SHAPE OF THE TRACK.

Is the track circular, oval, or lopsided? Is it wider at the front or wider at the back? Are the toes symmetrically or asymmetrically arranged?

STEP 2. COUNT THE NUMBER OF TOES.

Be careful—a lot can confound this seemingly simple task. Toes may not register clearly, or they may be set far off to the side. Stray marks may look like toes. Try to find multiple prints to verify your count.

STEP 3. LOOK AT THE CLAW MARKS.

Some animals have long stout claws, while others have short fine claws. Cats have retractable claws, which often do not show in their tracks at all.

STEP 4. MEASURE THE SIZE OF THE TRACK.

Measure the track's length and width. While animal foot sizes can vary tremendously within a species, track size will help you narrow down the possibilities.

HOW TO MEASURE TRACKS

Measure tracks along their longest and widest points. Measure length from the rear edge of the rearmost pad to the front edge of the foremost toe. Measure width across the widest part of the foot, including all of the toes. Look for clear tracks relatively free from distortion. If you can, measure several tracks to get an average. The measurements of mammal tracks in this guide do not include claws, except where they are indistinguishable from the toes. Measurements for bird and herp (reptiles and amphibians) tracks do include claws. Measurements for "game" and "webbed" bird tracks do not include the hallux (the rear-facing toe).

Gaits & Track Patterns

Gaits describe how an animal moves. Track patterns are the arrangement of footprints left by a particular gait. Most mammals and herps in the Northeast move on all fours, while birds walk on two legs, like us. Two-legged (bipedal) and four-legged (quadrupedal) gaits can each be divided into two broad categories: symmetric and asymmetric. Symmetric gaits have an even rhythm and produce lines of evenly spaced tracks or track pairs. Asymmetric gaits have an uneven rhythm, resulting in groups of tracks separated by distinct gaps.

BIPEDAL GAITS & TRACK PATTERNS

A symmetric bipedal gait is called a **walk** when the animal always has at least one foot on the ground. It is called a **run** if there is a moment when both feet are off the ground mid-stride. Both gaits produce a zigzagging line of tracks, with walks usually showing shorter steps and a wider trail than runs. Larger birds and those that spend lots of time on the ground usually walk or run.

Turkey walk

An asymmetric bipedal gait is called a **hop** when the animal jumps with both feet together, leaving side-by-side tracks. It's called a **skip** when the footfalls are staggered, resulting in offset pairs of tracks. Smaller perching birds typically hop or skip.

Crow skip

QUADRUPEDAL GAITS & TRACK PATTERNS

A quadrupedal **walk** is a symmetric gait in which the animal always has at least one front foot and one hind foot on the ground. With each step, the animal may place its hind foot on the ground either behind its front track (understep), on top of it (direct register), or in front of it (overstep). Raccoons use an extreme overstep, placing their hind foot next to the front track on the opposite side of the body. Walking is the most common gait for large rodents, "five-toed walkers," cats, deer, and most herps.

Coyote walk

A **trot** is the quadrupedal version of the bipedal run. The two legs diagonally opposite each other move at the same time, and there is a moment when the animal has all four feet off the ground. Similar to walks, trots can leave either direct register or overstep patterns. Overstep trots generally require the animal to turn its body slightly, allowing the hind feet to pass to the side of the front feet. Trots are the most common gaits for some tiny mammals, most dogs, and some lizards.

Fox trot

Lopes and Gallops are asymmetric gaits in which all four legs alternately gather and extend, creating distinct groupings of four tracks. In lopes and gallops, each foot moves independently. If the track pattern shows at least one hind foot landing even with or behind either front foot, it is generally called a lope. If both hind feet register ahead of both front feet in the group, it is generally called a gallop. Lopes are common gaits for skunks and larger weasels. Gallops are the fastest gaits used by most large carnivores and hoofed animals.

Skunk lope

Red Fox gallop

Hops and Bounds are similar to lopes and gallops, except the hind feet push off and land together. The resulting track patterns show hind tracks side-by-side, or nearly so. If the hind tracks register behind or partly behind the front ones, trackers call the gait a hop. Otherwise we call it a bound. Bounding animals' hind feet usually straddle their front feet, causing hind tracks to register wider. Smaller weasels use a modified "2x2 bound" in which their hind feet land directly in the front tracks. Hops and bounds usually produce more compact track groups than lopes and gallops, with larger spaces between groups. They are the most common gaits for frogs, many tiny mammals, squirrels, and rabbits. Many mammals bound when moving over rough terrain and use the "2x2 bound" in deep snow.

Squirrel bound

Weasel 2x2 bound

BIRD TRACK GROUPS

Most bird tracks in the Northeast fall into four categories, based on their overall shape.

Classic: Perching birds, diurnal raptors, and herons leave **classic** bird tracks showing three forward-facing toes and one similarly sized rear-facing toe, called the hallux. This is the most common bird track shape. Larger birds that leave classic tracks typically walk. Smaller species variously walk, run, skip, and hop.

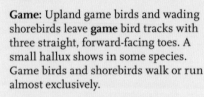

Zygodactyl: Woodpecker, owl, roadrunner, and parrot tracks have two toes pointing forward and two pointing backward. This track shape is called **zygodactyl**, meaning "paired toes." Woodpeckers typically hop. Owls walk.

Game: Upland game birds and wading shorebirds leave **game** bird tracks with three straight, forward-facing toes. A small hallux shows in some species. Game birds and shorebirds walk or run almost exclusively.

Webbed: Seabirds and waterfowl leave **webbed** tracks with three forward-facing toes and sometimes a small hallux. The outer toes in webbed tracks curve inward. Most waterfowl walk with their feet turned inward (oddly, the opposite of what we call "duck footed").

REPTILE & AMPHIBIAN TRACK GROUPS

Reptiles and amphibians, or herps, have different leg structures than mammals, leading them to shift side-to-side as they move, often twisting their feet and blurring their tracks. Because of this, and their habitats, clear tracks are less common than in birds or mammals. Herp tracks are difficult to identify beyond the order, but that's often enough. This guide shows examples of the tracks of each of the four orders of herps found in the Northeast.

Frogs and Toads frequently hop with their front feet facing in toward each other and their much larger hind feet registering wider, slightly farther back, and angled outward. On firm substrate, often only the tips of the toes of the hind feet register, forming a pair of "check marks." Toads have shorter, stouter toes than frogs and often walk as well as hop.

Salamanders and Newts walk on land, leaving small trails of closely spaced tracks surrounding a prominent body or tail drag. Most species have four clawless toes on their front feet and five on their larger hind feet, though some toes may be very small.

Lizards typically walk, trot, or bound, leaving trails similar to those of comparably sized mammals but usually less distinct. Tracks typically show five long, slender toes on each foot tipped with sharp claws. Many trails also include some trail drag.

Snake trail

Snakes, which are closely related to lizards, leave distinctive serpentine body marks without accompanying footprints.

Turtles and Tortoises walk exclusively, leaving wide trails with short steps. Tracks tend to be round or wider than long, and show prominent claw marks. They have five toes on each foot, but the outermost toe on the hind foot is reduced in many species and may not register.

Track Group Chart

Track Group	STEP 1: Overall Shape	STEP 2: # of Toes	STEP 3: Claws Show?	
TINY MAMMALS	Tracks generally well under 1"	4 (rodents) or 5 (others) front; 5 hind	Usually tiny dots. May be difficult to see	
SQUIRRELS	Long toes and a triangular-shaped palm	4 front; 5 hind	Fine. Usually register	
LARGE RODENTS	Long toes; hind tracks usually larger than front	4 front; 5 hind	Stout. May be indistinct from toes	
RABBITS	Egg-shaped; pads usually indistinct	5 front; 4 hind	Short, blunt. Often obscured by fur	
SKUNKS	Compact; stubby toes rarely splay	5 front & hind	Long and stout. Usually very prominent	
WEASELS	Large negative space between small toes and a chevron-shaped palm	5 front & hind	Fine. Usually visible	
DOGS	Oval, symmetrical. Large toes make up most of the track	4 front & hind	Usually register, but can be inconspicuous	
CATS	Round, asymmetrical fronts. Large palm makes up most of the track	4 front & hind	Sharp. Usually retracted, but can be prominent	
FIVE-TOE WALKERS	Often resemble human hand- or footprints	5 front & hind	Variable. May or may not show clearly	
UNGULATES	Round or heart-shaped hoof prints	1 (horses); 2 (others)	Dewclaws show at speed or in deep substrate	

Track Group Chart

Track Group	STEP 1: Arrangement of Toes	STEP 2: Shape of Toes	STEP 3: Webbing?	
CLASSIC BIRD	3 toes forward 1 toe back	Straight or curved	Sometimes at the base of the toes	
ZYGODAC-TYL BIRD	2 toes forward 2 toes back	Straight	None	
GAME BIRD	3 toes forward 0 or 1 smaller toe back	Straight	Sometimes at the base of the toes	
WEBBED BIRD	3 toes forward 0 or 1 smaller toe back	Outer toes curved	Yes, but may not register clearly	

Track Group	STEP 1: Overall Shape	STEP 2: # of Toes	STEP 3: Claws?	
FROGS & TOADS	Hind feet usually register as a pair of "check marks"	4 front; 5 hind	None, but toe tips resemble claw marks	
SALAMAN-DERS & NEWTS	Small, closely spaced tracks	4 front; 5 hind	None	
LIZARDS	Small. Long toes, but tracks usually indistinct	5 front; 5 hind	Typically slender. Often indistinct in tracks	
SNAKES	Serpentine body marks without footprints	None	None	
TURTLES & TORTOISES	Round to oval. May be wider than long	5 front; 5 hind (often only 4 register)	Long and stout. Often only claws register	

Adventure Quick Guides

Only Northeast Animal Tracks

Organized by group for quick and easy identification

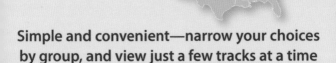

Simple and convenient—narrow your choices by group, and view just a few tracks at a time

- Pocket-size format—easier than laminated foldouts
- Realistic track illustrations with size information
- More than 60 mammal species—plus major groups of birds, reptiles, and amphibians
- Step-by-step guide to track identification
- Track information chart and sample track patterns

Get these *Adventure Quick Guides* for your area

NATURE / ANIMALS / NORTHEAST

ISBN 978-1-64755-076-9 $9.95 U.S.

PUBLICATIONS
Adventure
an imprint of AdventureKEEN